NORMA JE... BAKER OF TROY

Anne Carson

NORMA JEANE BAKER OF TROY

a version of Euripides's *Helen*

A NEW DIRECTIONS PAPERBOOK

Published by arrangement with Oberon Books, Ltd.

"Persephone" by Stevie Smith, copyright © 1950 by Stevie Smith.

Manufactured in the United States of America

First published as New Directions Paperbook 1467 in 2020

Library of Congress Cataloging-in-Publication
Names: Carson, Anne, 1950– author. | Euripides. Helen.
Title: Norma Jeane Baker of Troy :
a version of Euripides's Helen / Anne Carson.
Description: First New Directions edition. |
New York : New Directions Publishing, 2020.
Identifiers: LCCN 2019043444 (print) | LCCN 2019043445 (ebook) |
ISBN 9780811229364 (trade paperback) |
ISBN 9780811229371 (ebook)
Classification: LCC PS3553.A7667 N67 2020 (print) |
LCC PS3553.A7667 (ebook) | DDC 812/.54—dc23
LC record available at https://lccn.loc.gov/2019043444

2 4 6 8 10 9 7 5 3

New Directions Books are published for James Laughlin
by New Directions Publishing Corporation
80 Eighth Avenue, New York 10011

NORMA JEANE BAKER OF TROY

Commissioned by The Shed, New York
Alex Poots, Artistic Director and CEO

World premiere April 9, 2019
The Kenneth C. Griffin Theater

Enter NORMA JEANE BAKER.

Enter Norma Jeane Baker.

Prologue.

This is the Nile and I'm a liar.

Those are both true.

Are you confused yet?

The play is a tragedy. Watch closely now

how I save it from sorrow.

I expect you've heard of the Trojan War

and how it was caused by Norma Jeane Baker,

harlot of Troy.

Well, welcome to Public Relations.

That was all a hoax.

A bluff, a dodge, a swindle, a gimmick, a gem of a
stratagem.

The truth is,

a cloud went to Troy.

A cloud in the shape of Norma Jean Baker.

The gods arranged it, sort of.

They flew me to LA. Locked me in a suite of the
Chateau Marmont.

Told me to learn my lines for *Clash By Night*,

a film with Fritz Lang, the famous director.

That's enough about him.

Speaking of ignorant armies though,

that cloud scam fooled everyone.

Maybe a thousand Trojans died at Troy. I feel bad
about them.

I feel bad about me.

You know the phrase "box office poison"?

How to redeem the good name of Norma Jeane?

How to explain it all to Arthur?

My good husband Arthur,

king of Sparta and New York,

dear honourable, old-fashioned Arthur,

who led an army to Troy to win me back.

I am after all his most prized possession—the Greeks

value women less than pure gold

but slightly ahead of oxen, sheep or goats—

but also,

and more important,

Arthur is a man who believes in war.

Men standing shoulder to shoulder,

tempered in the fire of battle.

Himself

in a crested helmet,

his army rippling around him

like bees smelling honey.

Arthur gives thanks to the gods every day

for the precision of command,

which makes order of the anarchy of his heart.

A cloud? he'll say. We went to Troy to get a cloud?

We lived all those years knee-deep in death for the
    sake of a cloud?

I'm not sure he'll believe me.

I'm not sure I believe me.

Just think,

when the Greeks first beached their ships at Troy

they could see the legendary city glittering a mere
football field away.

It took them ten years to walk to it.

A thousand bloody T-shirts left on the sand.

Oh I need a drink.

Or a big bowl of whipped cream. I've got to think.

NORMA JEANE *sits, takes out her knitting.*

~~~~~~~~~~~~~~~~~~~~~~~~~~~~~~~~~~~~~~

εἴδωλον

"image, likeness, simulacrum, replica, proxy, idol"

HISTORY OF WAR: LESSON 1

To make people believe that a replica is the real thing, manipulate "the optics" of the situation. Managing optics cleverly will generate an alternate version of the facts, which then stands alongside the facts like a cloud in the shape of a woman, or a golden Hollywood idol in place of a mousy-haired pinup girl from Los Angeles.

CASE STUDY: The Russian military now uses decoy armaments of a Euripidean design—lifesize tanks, MiG-31 fighter jets and missile launchers made of inflatable plastic. A hot-air balloon company provides them to the Ministry of Defense.

FALLOUT: There may be ethical queries. Point out that war has always made use of camouflage, spies, stealth tactics. Make it clear: completely convincing unreal weapons able to pop up or vanish in moments are too good to forego! Do not use terms like "trickery" or "deceit." Substitute the playful and musical Russian expression *maskirovka*: "masking."

APPLICATIONS (specific): Move Helen's mask aside momentarily if she wants to spit tequila in your mouth.

APPLICATIONS (general): Trust Euripides. Trust Helen. She never went to Troy. Marilyn really was a blonde. And we all go to heaven when we die. As Marilyn used to say, "Keep the balloon and dare not to worry."

~~~~~~

NORMA JEANE continues knitting.

Episode One.

Enter Greek sailor trying to find his way home from Troy.

Sailor sees me, does one of those (doubletakes).

Says he can't believe how much I look like *her*.

Thought he'd never see a pair of tits like those again.

Like *these*. Again.

Goes into a rant about Norma Jeane Baker the harlot of Troy—

that WMD in the forked form of woman! He curses her! He spits on her!

He calls the gods to spit on her!

And so forth.

I let him unload it all.

Then ask about his family

(usually where the anger starts).

Turns out his brother suicided at Troy

and their dad holds him responsible.

Don't bother coming home alone, said Dad.

And I thought, *Fuck! Those humans!*

Always finding a way to break each other's hearts!

But anyway then we got back to talking of Troy

and Norma Jeane, whom

he was absolutely sure he'd seen on the last day at
    Troy

being dragged off by the hair,

as clear as I see you, he says.

Who dragged her? I says.

Her own husband, he says, Arthur of New York and
    Sparta.

And next thing he tells me—heartbreak!—is

Arthur might not be coming back!

Rumour has it

Arthur's lost his way sailing home from Troy with
    Norma Jeane.

Assumed dead.

Who'll save me from Fritz Lang now?

Exit NORMA JEANE.

~~~~~~

τραῦμα

"wound"

HISTORY OF WAR: LESSON 2

War creates two categories of persons: those who outlive it and those who don't.

Both carry wounds.

CHANGING ATTITUDES: An ancient Homeric catalogue of battlefield trauma would include wounds to eyeball, nose, palate, forehead, throat, collarbone, back of skull, nape of neck, upper arm, forearm, heart, lungs, liver, spleen, thigh, knee, shin, heel, ankle. Lasting psychological damage, however keen a concern of modern research, does not seem to have interested the ancient poet.

CONTINUITIES: On the other hand, Homer has given us Achilles, who went berserk in the midst of battle (*Iliad*) and Odysseus, who went berserk afterwards (*Odyssey*), while Euripides makes a hero out of Helen, who was brutalized by merely staring at war too long.

TEACHABLE MOMENTS: In Euripides' play *Helen*, we watch Helen watch her husband, Menelaos, as he ambushes and slaughters a boatload of unarmed people. She cheers him on, shouting, "Where is the glory of Troy? Show it to these barbarians!"

DISCUSSION TOPICS: Compare and contrast catching a spear in the spleen with utter mental darkness. Consider ancient *vs* modern experience. Consider whether any of these is what is meant in poetry by "a beautiful death."

~~~~~~~~~~~~~~~~~~~~~~~~~~~~~~~~~~~~~~~

Enter NORMA JEANE.

Enter Norma Jeane as Mr. Truman Capote.

First choral song.

Enter chorus.

I am my own chorus.

I think of my chorus as Mr. Truman Capote.

He was a good friend, he told me the truth.

You'll never admit it when you've made a mess,

he said to me once

and that was true.

I can still hear his funny little girl voice—Truman

had a voice like a negligee, always

slipping off one bare shoulder,

just a bit.

And he hated melodrama,

though he loved to quote poetry—highbrow
   stuff—

here's one he says is about me—

by Stevie Smith (it's called "Persephone"):

> *I am that Persephone*
> *Who played with her darlings in Sicily*
> *Against a background of social security.*
>
> *Oh what a glorious time we had.*
> *Or had we not? They said it was sad.*
> *I was born good, grown bad.*

And isn't that how it always starts, this myth that
   ends with the girl "grown bad"?

She's in a meadow gathering flowers

twirling her own small sunny hours.

When up rides a man on black horses.

Up rides a man in a black hat.

Up rides a man with a black letter to deliver.

Shall I make you my queen?

She's maybe 12 or 13.

Rape

is the story of Helen,

Persephone,

Norma Jeane,

Troy.

War is the context

and God is a boy.

Oh my darlings,

they tell you you're born with a precious pearl.

Truth is,

it's a disaster to be a girl.

> *Up came the black horses and the dark King.*
> *And the harsh sunshine was as if it had never been.*
> *In the halls of Hades they said I was queen.*

Exit NORMA JEANE *as Mr. Truman Capote.*

~~~~~~~~~~~~~~~~~~~~~~~~~~~~~~~~~~~~

ἁρπάζειν

"to take"

HISTORY OF WAR: LESSON 3

If you pick a flower, if you snatch a handbag, if you possess a woman, if you plunder a storehouse, ravage a countryside or occupy a city, you are a *taker*. You are *taking*. In ancient Greek you use the verb ἁρπάζειν, which comes over into Latin as *rapio, rapere, raptus sum* and gives us English *rapture* and *rape*—words stained with the very early blood of girls, with the very late blood of cities, with the hysteria of the end of the world. Sometimes I think language should cover its own eyes when it speaks.

~~~~~~~~~~~~~~~~~~~~~~~~~~~~~~~~~~~~

Enter NORMA JEANE.

Enter Norma Jeane as Norma Jeane.

Episode two.

The story so far:

TROY DOWN

THOUSANDS DEAD

NORMA JEANE TO BLAME

NORMA JEANE NOT TO BLAME

ARTHUR LOST (AT SEA)

NORMA JEANE CAPTIVE (CHATEAU MARMONT)

EXIT MR. TRUMAN CAPOTE TO LUNCH WITH MISS PEARL BAILEY

NORMA JEANE sits, knits a bit, puts down knitting.

(Here's an aside.

I'm not generally a weeping woman

but the sailor told me

a bit of news

I didn't mention before. About my daughter,

my dear one, back in New York.

What he heard is that

she's dropped out of school

and is hoarding her meds.

Hermione's her name.

She must be 17 now.

A golden flower of a girl.

A precarious girl.

I've wanted to call her so many times—Fritz Lang
    said *No*—

we can't jeopardize the cloud scam.

MGM has a lot invested in this war at Troy,

even beside the movie deals there's spinoffs, casinos,
    reality shows.

But Hermione!

Hermione is my own soul walking around in another body.

So here's what I do when I really miss her.

I use the wind telephone.

A guy in Japan—remember that place in Japan where they had the big wave,

the earthquake? and the sea

came up over the town, thousands drowned.

And the ones left behind

were so sad they couldn't live.

So this guy buys himself an old telephone booth,

sets it up by the side of the road

on the edge of town.

People can go in and dial a number

and talk to the dead, talk to their lost ones, talk to the underworld.

It's rotary dial.

People find that comforting.

Most of them just say *Hi Dad* or *Funny weather these days* or *Guess what we got a dog*—

but they come out of the booth smiling.

It was said in the town that the phone sometimes rang

at odd hours.

I've no opinion on that.)

Exit NORMA JEANE *on wind phone, hand to ear,*
Hermione it's me, hello hello hello hello hello.

Enter NORMA JEANE.

Enter Norma Jeane.

Episode three.

Surprise!

Enter Arthur.

I was downstairs chatting up the night clerk, Bobby.

Arthur just came walking into the lobby.

Looking like a bum. Smelling like a guy who's spent
    7 years in the same shirt.

I tell you who was more surprised than me, however,

was he.

No, he said.

No, he said eleven more times.

I'll skip ahead.

He told me his Troy story—

basically nine years of cattle raids and pillaging the
locals (Arthur calls it Blood, Sheep and Tears).

Then, year ten, Achilles wakes up and they take the
town.

Kill all the men,

rape all the women,

pack up the boats and sail for home.

Main point being: he got his war prize, the whole
reason he went, his *casus belli,*

his Norma Jeane

(or so he thinks).

He said she was there,

locked in a bathroom,

kind of high.

Had to break her nose with his fist but he got her.

Then they wandered seven years through stormy seas

and alien airports, washed up yesterday on Venice
Beach.

Where's Norma Jeane now? I said and he said, Best
Western.

Okay, I said. *My turn.*

Okay, I said, my turn.

I said that twice. Nervous.

So.

I explain to Arthur about the cloud.

A cloud went to Troy, I say. It wasn't me.

MGM had the rights to a war movie, big investors
   involved, you know

how things work.

That Norma Jeane at Troy, *that wasn't me* (I repeat).
   It was a cloud.

He stands there like a stilled avalanche.

Cloud, he says.

We fought ten years at Troy over a cloud.

Well, I said, that's the gist.

And then,

this is God's truth,

Arthur burst into flame.

I extinguished Arthur by beating him with my
   bathrobe.

Just then his phone rang.

It was the manager at the Best Western.

Arthur of New York and Sparta?

Yes.

Room 7B?

Yes.

It's about your wife.

My wife?

The maid went in with towels,

handed them to your wife and

your wife melted into thin air—you know what I'm saying? She

dematerialized. Beamed out. Right before Maria's eyes.

I got a hysterical maid here and you're still paying double occupancy.

~~~~~~~~~~~~~~~~~~~~~~~~~~~~~~~~~~

δουλεία

"slavery"

HISTORY OF WAR: LESSON 4

The economy of ancient Greece, like that of early modern America, depended on the institution of slavery. And warfare was a factory for the production of slaves. Anyone who survived a war on the losing side was destined for this category. Because ancient slavery was not predicated on any pseudoscience of genetic inferiority, kings and queens and movie stars, as well as bakers and barbers, were in theory but a city's fall away from servitude—Helen being a legendary example of that rare creature who could talk or charm or seduce her way out of this fate. Surely all the other fine ladies of Troy ended up slaves of some Greek soldier or his wife at home. Helen evidently persuaded her husband, dear honourable old-fashioned Menelaos, king of Sparta, to reinstate her as wife and queen, although technically, legally and hygienically she was dirt.

BEAUTY AND JUSTICE: Some women know how to keep the game going, some don't. When Marilyn Monroe did telephone interviews the journalist would often begin by asking, "So, Marilyn, what do you have on?" And she would answer, "The radio."

~~~~~~~~~~~~~~~~~~~~~~~~~~~~~~~~~~

NORMA JEANE takes up knitting.

One thing I learned from psychoanalysis is how to fake it, with men. The guy I went to, Dr. Cheeseman—one day we were talking about Arthur's dimpled white buttocks and how I felt no sexual attraction for them or for him, which was awkward as we were newlywed and Arthur, king of Sparta and New York, hoped to engender a tiny prince Arthur—and Dr. Cheeseman went into his Lacanian riff, about how "desire full stop is always desire of the Other capital O", which I took to mean "visualize Yves Montand when screwing Arthur" but that didn't work for me and what did work for me, oddly enough, was when I found myself one day describing Arthur to Dr. Cheeseman as an Asian boy— Asian boys being Dr. Cheeseman's own little problem—and so discovering Arthur to be desirable by seeing him shine back at me from Dr. Cheeseman's eyes. Is this too weird? I don't think it's uncommon.

Psychoanalysts call it triangular desire. But it's not what most people mean by faking it. They just mean acting. Well, in the first place, acting is not fake. And, number two, acting has nothing to do with desire. Desire is about vanishing. You dream of a bowl of cherries and next day receive a letter written in red juice. Or, a better example: you know I'm not a totally *bona fide* blonde—I always say *blonde on the inside is what counts*—so I get a bit of colour every 2 weeks from a certain Orlando in Brentwood and I used to wonder *shouldn't I dye the hair down there too*, you know, make it match, but the thing is—talk about a bowl of cherries—most men like it dark. Most men like what slips away. A bit of strange. But I digress.

The manager at Best Western was still talking

when Arthur closed the phone

and closed his eyes and said,

I need a drink.

Good idea, I said.

I need to think.

Exit NORMA JEANE.

~~~~~~

παλλακή

"concubine"

HISTORY OF WAR: LESSON 5

How do you define dirt? Here is what the ancient Greeks thought of it: dirt is matter out of place. The poached egg on your plate at breakfast is not dirt. The poached egg on page 202 of the Greek lexicon in the library of the British Museum is dirt. Dirt is something that has crossed a boundary it ought not to have crossed. Dirt confuses categories and mixes up form.

APPLICATIONS: Use this spatial hygiene to explain certain neo-liberal neuroses. Because the spooky thing about dirt, if you're a neo-liberal, is that dirt is not passive. Dirt is coming to get you.

CASE STUDY: The noun for "concubine" in Greek comes from the verb that means "to sprinkle." A concubine is a stranger who sprinkles herself into someone else's household—as Helen does when she follows Paris to Troy—hoping to assimilate herself to the texture there. Helen does not belong in the house of Priam. She comes in tracking Greek mud all over the floor.

CAN YOU PASS: Assimilation is tricky. You have to invent a new self in a new household. Even Marilyn Monroe had trouble at the start. "When I signed my first autograph I had to go slow. I wasn't too sure where the 'y' went or where you put the 'i.'"

TEACHABLE MOMENT: Helen's very first appearance in history and literature, at verse 126–129 of the third book of Homer's *Iliad*, shows her sitting in her chamber in the palace of Priam, weaving. She is weaving a vast tapestry that depicts, minute by minute, the battle going on outside her window. Notice Homer uses the verb "sprinkle" to describe how she embroiders the dooms of men into her web. Helen knows dirt. Helen is a death-sprinkler.

BATTLEFIELD CLICHÉ: Her thread is deep dark red.

~~~~~~~~~~~~~~~~~~~~~~~~~~~~~~~~~~~~~~~

Enter NORMA JEANE *on wind phone, hand to ear.*

Dear Hermione,

I dreamed of you.

I saw you floating face down.

Every day is a struggle here, I woke up late

and had a bad thought:

all those lives at Troy, all those souls gone down to
   Hades for my sake—

who pays for that?

It wouldn't be some sort of capital obligation would
   it? Some kind of debt

that needs to be made good?

Surely the life of a girl can't be *collateral*?

Surely the gods don't think like that?

How do gods think?

Does it all make sense to them—war? Clouds?
  Fakery? People in flames?

Do they like a good war show? Cover their eyes

at the bloody parts?

Poor gods!

We're beyond that.

We don't cover our eyes anymore, do we—we
  mortals, we creatures of a day?

We're more or less blind—

shooting day for night.

And anyway, a heart surgeon told me once,

no need to worry: once the cutting starts,

a wound

shines by its own light.

Exit NORMA JEANE.

Enter NORMA JEANE as Mr. Truman Capote.

Second choral ode.

We have three objectives.

One: rescue this play from melodrama.

Two: keep her away from that wind phone.

And three (plotwise):

get Arthur out of Hollywood alive.

MGM thinks him already dead, they've sent out

advance PR for the reality show (I think Orson
Welles wrote it).

I'll give you the premise:

Norma Jeane's married Fritz Lang.

They bought the Chateau Marmont, put in a race-
track.

Fritz took a physics course at Pomona and won the
    Nobel Prize.

But he lost all his horses in a fire set by the Taliban.

Norma Jeane's decided to join the Taliban

and is training as a prophet.

Each show ends with a prophet's round table —

they bring in local prophets, all vote Yes or No

on who's better at holding hot coals in their mouth,

Norma Jeane or Fritz.

No room in any of this for Arthur,

obviously.

No room for Norma Jeane's tortured personal truth
    either.

I love her dearly but — let's be frank —

there's nothing mythic here.

She's just a bit of grit caught in the world's need for
    transcendence.

It's a hustle. I keep telling her:

lower your eyes,

count to four,

raise your eyes,

say the line.

That's how you lock in a hustle.

Make them feel they're looking at Norma Jeane
nude

even if you're standing there with all your clothes
on.

Exit Norma Jeane as Mr. Truman Capote.

Exit NORMA JEANE.

~~~~~~~~~~~~~~~~~~~~~~~~~~~~~~~~~~~~~~~

ἀπάτη

"deception illusion trickery duplicity doubleness
fraud bluff beguilement hankypanky dodge hood-
wink artifice chicanery subterfuge ruse hoax shift
stratagem swindle guile wile wiles The Wiles of
Woman"

HISTORY OF WAR: LESSON 6

In war, things go wrong. Blame Woman.

YOU LOSE YOU WIN YOU WIN YOU LOSE: The
wiles of woman cause men much anger, an anger
amounting to agony. Their whoring is a big yellow tree
that blooms in a man's mind, it is agony. Is she human?
Are you? Is she a beast out of control? There's so much
danger. No human can become *just a beast*, you plunge
beyond—beyond what? Remember Jack the Ripper?
"I'm down on whores and I shan't quit ripping them till
I get buckled," Jack wrote in a letter to the newspaper,
September 18, 1888. He never did get buckled. Of
course insane, his mind blooming with it, who could
go down that rabbit hole or unlock such a puzzle as
Jack?—but still, the woman! the thing is! the woman
has everything and you smile and you take some.

I GOT THIS FROM TED HUGHES AND WHO
SHOULD KNOW IF NOT TED HUGHES: Of eve-
rything she has you have absolutely nothing, she has
everything too much, so you take some. At first just a
little. It blooms. You smile. You are in agony.

~~~~~~~~~~~~~~~~~~~~~~~~~~~~~~~~~~~~~~

Enter NORMA JEANE.

Enter Norma Jeane as Norma Jeane.

Okay. Hustle on.

Episode four.

Here's how it goes.

I was supposed to tell the producers that Truman
   and I had to go to New York

for the weekend.

Say we'd take Dr. Cheeseman along to keep me off
   the booze.

Substitute Arthur for Cheeseman at the last minute.

Of course they'd ask, Why go to New York?

Truman said, Use Hermione.

She's a good pretext.

The overdose. The coma.

Everyone's heard about it.

Say you don't know when you'll be back,

there might be a funeral,

there might not.

I put the burning coals in my mouth

and I said this.

Then I fainted.

> *I am that Persephone*
> *Who played with her darlings in Sicily*
> *Against a background of social security.*
>
> *Oh what a glorious time we had.*
> *Or had we not? They said it was sad.*
> *I was born good, grown bad.*

~~~~~~

βάρβαρος

"barbarian, Other"

HISTORY OF WAR: LESSON 7

Barbarians always come from somewhere uncanny, on the far side of No Man's Land or an ocean or the fence. They are another species. They have different, more savage helmets and backpacks with animal hair on them. Their bread is black, their smell heavy or ancient, their parapets bizarre—they build them up with cooking pots, pillow slips, anything! Even the barbs of their barbed wire look more numerous and foreign. There's no doubt about it, they're a dirty lot of bastards.

WHOM SHALL WE DRINK TO: Ancient Greeks gave the name *barbaros* to anyone not provably or originally a Greek. The word is thought to replicate the sound made by sheep: *bar bar bar bar.*

~~~~~~

Episode five.

When I woke it was night and already pouring.

Pouring what? That's not rain.

Aristotle thought earthquakes were caused

by winds trapped in subterranean caves.

We're more scientific now, we know

it's just five guys fracking the fuck out of the world
while it's still legal.

Miss Pearl Bailey came in, said, Truman sent me,

Arthur's getting a boat. Time to exit the Chateau
Marmont.

We'll walk down—

that sound you hear is debris pouring in the elevator
shaft.

So we walked down, seventeen floors.

Earthquake light is bizarre, like morning at mid-
night.

I could hear the voices of birds going round and
round

looking for a back door.

Everywhere the crunch of glass underfoot.

And Miss Pearl Bailey was tilting—no, the hotel
was—all

top seven floors snapped off, billowed sideways

and crashed.

A sudden rush of open sky made us look up—tenth
floor—and laugh.

It was a photoelectric laugh.

Last laugh that day.

Arthur's boat is a medium-sized trireme, same kind
he took to Troy.

(I never went to Troy, *that was a cloud*, don't forget
this.)

By now you could see the wave coming up Sunset
Boulevard.

A single wave filling Sunset Boulevard with white
and black foam five stories high.

Arthur and Truman were packing the boat

with all the kitchen and wait staff of the hotel,

plus Pearl's entourage,

a mob of anorexic youth in sexual T-shirts.

The wave hit.

The night roared.

We were popped up to the top of the sky and we set
    off. Sailing east.

~~~~~~~~~~~~~~~~~~~~~~~~~~~~~~~~~~~~~

καιρός

"opportunity"

HISTORY OF WAR: LESSON 8

Think about bronze. It was the Bronze Age when the
war at Troy took place (if it took place at all). Killing
a man in full bronze armour—helmet, breastplate,
greaves—was not an easy task. Two relatively small
targets affording maximum bloody access were the
neck and the groin, i.e. exposed areas at the top
and bottom of the breastplate. A person wounded
there would bleed out in a few hours. But for instant
certain death you would aim your sword or spear
or arrow or sharpened stick at the place where the
helmet stopped above the eyes, the temple of the
head. These three locations were called *καιρία*, mortal
spots, from the Greek *καιρός*, which means "the exact
right place and time for something to happen, the
critical juncture, the perfect opportunity."

NOT YET IRONY: Notice καιρός has its accent on the
final syllable. This same word with accent moved to the
initial syllable, καῖρος, was a technical term from the art
of weaving to indicate the thrums of the web or, more
specifically, that critical point in space and time when
the weaver must thrust her thread through a gap that
momentarily opens in the warp of the cloth.

TEACHABLE MOMENT: We have already reflected on Helen's first appearance in Homer's *Iliad* (Book III, verses 126–129) where she sits in her room live-streaming the war at Troy onto a tapestry. Her thread weaves in and out of living skulls.

~~~~~~~~~~~~~~~~~~~~~~~~~~~~~~~~~~~~~

Hear that? Living skulls! What are we doing here?
What war at Troy? Does anyone care? Gods of love
and hate! Aren't they the same god? All of us, all our
lives, searching for the one perfect enemy—you,
me, Helen, Paris, Menelaos, all those crazy Greeks!
all those hapless Trojans! my dear beloved Jack! Jack
and I fought all the time. I remember almost noth-
ing but the fights—every fight a war to end all wars,
you know how it goes, a righteous war, a final war,
the worst fight you've ever had, you can't do this
again, this time you'll get things straight one way
or the other or it's over, he'll see what you mean,
see you're right, fights aren't about anything except
being right, are they? once and for all. You feel old.
Wrong. Clumsy. You sit in two chairs on the porch.
Or the kitchen. Or the front hall. Hell arrives. It's
as if the war was already there, waiting, the two of
you poured into it like wet concrete. The chairs you

sit in are the wrong chairs, they're the chairs you never sit in because they're so uncomfortable, you keep thinking you should move but you don't, your neck hurts, you hate your neck, evening closes in. Birds move about the yard. Hell yawns. War pours out of both of you, steaming and stinking. You rush backward from it and become children, every sentence slamming you back into the child you still are, every sentence not what you meant to say at all but the meaning keeps contracting, or flaring, or flaring and contracting, as sparks drop on gasoline, *Fuckshit this! Fuckshit that*! no reason to live. You're getting vertigo. He's being despicable. Your mother was like this. Stop whimpering. No use asking, *What is this about?* Don't leave the room. I have to leave the room. Breathless, blaming, I'm not blaming! How is this not blaming! Hours pass or do they. You say the same things or are they different things? Hell smells stale. Fights aren't about anything, fights are about themselves. You're stiff. You hate these chairs. Nothing is resolved. It is too dark to see. You both go to bed and doze slightly, touching slightly. In the night a nightmare. Some giant bird, or insect, some flapping thing, trying to settle on the back of your neck, you can't see what it is or get it off. Pure fear. Scream unearthly. He jerks you awake. Oh sweetie, he says. He is using his inside voice, his most inside voice. The distance between that voice and the fight voice measures your whole world. How can a voice change so. You are saved. He has saved you. He sees you saved. An easement occurs, as night dew on leaves. And yet (you think suddenly) you yourself do not possess this sort of inside voice—no wonder he's lonely. You cannot offer this refuge, cannot save him, not ever, and, although physiological in origin, or genetic, or who knows, you understand the lack is felt by him as a turning away. No one can heal this. You both decide without words to just—skip it. You grip one another. In the night, in the silence, the grip slowly loosens and silence washes you out somewhere onto a shore of sleep.

Morning arrives. Troy is still there. You hear from below the clatter of everyone putting on their armour. You go to the window.

~~~~~~

τις, τίς

"someone, anyone, a person, a certain person, who?"

HISTORY OF WAR: LESSON 9

τις the indefinite, τίς the interrogative, pronoun of
ancient Greek. It might sound to you like almost the
same word, but for the accent—that slight upward
pitch? Easy words, easy to learn, easy to slide around.
Easy to slide "interrogative" sideways into "indefinite"
or downward into "definite" (say) enemy—*who is that
at the door?* Is it someone we know? Is it one of them?
Were they here yesterday? The ones camping on
the shore? The ones who took our soup? Took our
cow? Took our doorstep? What do they want with
doorsteps? What do they want with our daughter?
Will any daughter do? Someone else's? Anyone? A
certain who. A certain melody. Any melody. A certain
pointed blade. Some blade. Some blunder. Some bar-
gain. Some bloody marriage. Some stupid obsession.
Some berserk battlefield anger. Some pretext for
war. Any pretext. Any daughter. Someone is anyone
is war is *who is that at the door?* Even among these
there are differing, there is any, there's a white cloth
on their, for whom no relatives have yet, a certain rate
of decomposition stuns you! a certain stink! a certain
stink of battlefields, any battlefield, *who's that at the
door?* Who's that stiff white blossom at the end of

your pointed blade, you who abandoned me here, who's that corpse of a girl now bloated to the size of a grown man—is anyone growing a man? Is that what we're growing here? Does a certain injury to the man distort the face beyond recognition, he could be anyone? Could be her? Who? Who are we deciding to kill now? What is that stain spreading from your neck to your knees to your doorstep to your ridiculous glass-like soul that was supposed to outlast the centuries, outlive the galaxies, survive the rules of love, master the odds of war and transcend all seven level oceans of Homer?

~~~~~~~~~~~~~~~~~~~~~~~~~~~~~~~~~~~~

NORMA JEANE as NORMA JEANE.

Inside me now I am empty of everything and every thought except Hermione. Hermione will meet us in New York at the pier, I say to myself. Hermione is not lying under a sheet in a beeping overlit emergency room. Hermione will run towards us, laughing and skeptical, with her coat undone. I keep trying to focus on her running with her coat undone, as she always did, and me reaching to close it, as I always did, me doing up a button and her pulling away exasperated, undoing it. Doing it, undoing it, doing it, undoing it, doing, undoing, doing, undoing, doing—like some crazed German expressionist film from the '30s—

I get out my knitting.

People laugh when I say it keeps me sane.

What are you knitting? says Miss Pearl Bailey.

She is eating almonds from a ziplock bag.

The fall of Troy, I say.

Big theme, she says.

Yes, and I'm putting in every detail.

Every blade of grass on Priam's lawn,

every lick of wind on a warrior's cheek,

every thin brown bat that whistled past the Greek
tents at dusk,

every fly that buzzed over their shit,

every pointless prayer,

every opaque oracle,

every bone that broke

in the baby they tossed over the wall on the last day.

Just then there's thunder.

Flashes of lightning shoot up from water to sky.

Hello Dolly! cries Miss Pearl.

Somewhere a doorbell rings.

We are sailing past car seats

and drowned cats and medicine.

I see all the sofas from the hotel lobby and a horse
     swimming.

I see suitcases and bicycle chains and a display case
     full of cheeses,

a display case full of smoked meats and fish, pillows,
     backpacks,

Bibles, a STOP sign, a Santa hat, people.

Dead people.

Some alive.

Some try to claw their way up onto our boat,

I beat them off with a boat hook.

They are not Hermione,

they are disqualified.

Final choral ode.

Enter Norma Jeane as Mr. Truman Capote to join
     Norma Jeane as Norma Jeane .

The night is golden now.

Maybe dawn is breaking somewhere.

Miss Pearl Bailey has started to sing in a low voice,

as we sail,

as we sail,

as we sail,

under no stars at all,

on.

> *Up came the black horses and the dark King.*
> *And the harsh sunshine was as if it had never been.*
> *In the halls of Hades they said I was queen.*

Exeunt omnes singing.